PANIC, ATTACK, U.S.A.

NATE, SLAWSON

for ♥

CONTENTS

i   Foreword by Peter Markus

THE TEENAGE SONNETS

7   YOU ARE SAXOPHONE

8   YOU ARE EMILY VALENTINE

9   YOU ARE THE SCENERY

10   YOU ARE AMPLIFIER

11   YOU ARE A FISH

12   YOU ARE NO DEPRESSION

13   YOU ARE A RIVER

14   YOU ARE JOHNNY LAWRENCE

15   YOU ARE LUNCH HOUR REVENGE THERAPY

16   YOU ARE ZOOEY DESCHANEL

17   YOU ARE CINCINNATI, OH

18   YOU ARE A BRIEF MEDITATION ON A SHORT STORY

19   YOU ARE MAGIC 8-BALL

20   YOU ARE A CAROUSEL

21   YOU ARE THE RATIO OF VAMPIRES TO RASPBERRIES

PANIC ATTACK, USA

25   THE DRUGSTORE IS A VOLCANO

26   LETTER WRITTEN IN BLOWTORCH

27   O SHOTGUN

28   MY B-SIDE IS SENTIMENTAL

29   SIX FLAGS PANIC ATTACK

31   ODE TO YOUR COOL HANDS

32   LET'S GET OLD TIME RELIGION

33   I BECOME TRACK FIVE ON MY AFGHAN WHIGS MIXTAPE

34   100,000 FIREFLIES (SUPERCHUNK COVER VERSION)

35   STRING THEORY

36   I AM THE TOPOGRAPHY

37   ODE TO A GIRL NAMED TELEVISION

38   MY STUPID HAIR IS SO 1992

39   WE ARE ALL THE ANIMALS

41   THE FIELD TRIP

42   WE ARE A MAP OF THE MIDWEST

45   MY BAND WILL BE NAMED YOUR NAME

ESSAYS FOR A BROKEN HEART

57   AN ESSAY ABOUT BLACK KEYS

58   AN ESSAY ABOUT GOSPEL MUSIC

60   AN ESSAY ABOUT RIVERS

62   AN ESSAY ABOUT FACTORIES

64   AN ESSAY ABOUT BENZODIAZEPINES

66   AN ESSAY ABOUT THE UNIVERSE

68   AN ESSAY ABOUT TOMMY GUNS

70   AN ESSAY ABOUT CAMERON FRYE

72   AN ESSAY ABOUT EVANGELICALISM

74   AN ESSAY ABOUT COCA-COLA

76   AN ESSAY ABOUT CINEMASCOPE

78   AN ESSAY ABOUT 21ST CENTURY POETRY

VERY VERY AGORAPHOBIA

83   GREAT WHITE SHARK

85   WHAT I MEAN IS YES

86   THE GALAXIE 500 POEM

88   BIRTHDAY POEM

90   THE LETTER I AM WRITING YOU NOW

92   JULY 4

93   JULY 4

94   JULY 4

95   WHEN YOU WERE A RABBIT

96   YOUR FUTURE LIFE

97   NOTHING MATTERS WHEN WE'RE GLOWING

98   BIRTHDAY POEM

100   IF I COULD FUCK A LANDSCAPE

Foreword by Peter Markus

Thank the poetry gods that there is someone like Nate Slawson in this otherwise neutered world. Thank the poetry gods that Nate Slawson writes with a hard-on. When I picture in my head what the speakers in these poems look like, this is what I come up with: a man naked on a pogo stick hopping down the street. This is a man, in other words, who lets everything hang out. This is a man who is not afraid or ashamed to tell it like it is. Christ if I don't wish there were more people like this, and especially more poets like this. I don't know the Nate Slawson who is a father and a husband and a son. I met him once in Chicago at a reading at Danny's Tavern. He was, as I remember him, quiet and maybe even awkwardly shy, with a thick full beard like the beard that hockey players sport in the thick of the playoffs, glasses too big for his face, with some sort of a hat pulled down almost over his eyes. He looked, in short, like a man in disguise. It's clear to me now that the other Nate Slawson—the Slawson of these poems—was hiding behind those eyes, that pulled-down hat, the face full of hair. I don't doubt that Nate Slawson is a good man, a good neighbor, well-liked by the people who have no idea that he writes poetry. But I think it's safe to say that Nate Slawson is nothing like the in-your-face speakers that are living large

i

and unquietly in the tiny chambers of these highly-charged and lyrical love poems. I like it when this happens, when a poet becomes other-than who he might otherwise be—Jekyll vs. Hyde—when he picks up a pencil and through this otherness, through the possibilities of language and sensation, becomes more than what his own life allows him to be.

These are poems that don't simply tell us what it's like to live. These are poems that tell us what it means to be alive. To be alive and to be thunderous inside a body and a skin that cannot contain the largeness and the wildness of the human heart. It's a heart, inside these poems, that is volcanic in its desire to not be alone. I am most often alone and yes, sometimes even lonely, when I most often reach for a book of poems. These poems by Nate Slawson make me feel less alone in this world. These poems make me feel limp and lukewarm next to the speakers who lurch out from under these pages. These speakers reach out and take us by the scruff of the neck, they cuff us upside the sides of our head, they shake their fists in our face and demand that we wake up, that we live as hungrily as the voices that breathe their heated breaths all over us and into our ears.

PANIC ATTACK, U.S.A.

The gentle are curious, but the curious / are not gentle.
—Frank O'Hara

I just don't know what I'm supposed to be.
—Charlotte, *Lost in Translation*

When will our fucking hearts cease to riot?
—Superchunk

TEENAGE SONNETS

YOU ARE SAXOPHONE

Is not your soul
a tiny jukebox
a pain in your heart
sprung from the
blues & which
when I cup my
hand to your chest
be like thunderous
rain like wasps in
a coffee can & thou
nettles & dry river-
bed thou sermon
of fire sister & we
hymnal of matchsticks?

YOU ARE EMILY VALENTINE

I know I promised you
I wouldn't make a scene
in front of all your friends
but is it wrong if I write
your name on the soles
of my tennis shoes is it
wrong if I want to stand
next to you in gym class
your legs remind me of
a Bruce Springsteen song
I would do a hundred sit-
ups for you & whisper your
name every time & kiss my
knees pretending they are you.

YOU ARE THE SCENERY

I promise I can keep
a secret for forever
you can whisper me
real slow if the moon
between your thighs
makes you feverish
or dark purple plumage
I got a note for you that
says *Can I bite your bottom
lip? Please check yes or no.*
I would like to bite your
bottom lip I would like
to bite your bottom lip
like it's all of Appalachia.

YOU ARE AMPLIFIER

I hope this don't sound
nothing like a prison love
letter but I wanna play with
your microphone sing
Something Else by The Kinks
from beginning to end
into your red red knees
& when I'm finished I'll be
your fuckin bass drum &
you can kick out the side
of my head, then cradle me
baby rabbit-like all Jackie O
how goddamn sweet is that
how killer would that be?

YOU ARE A FISH

There's a treehouse in my
backyard I like to sit in
when it's cold & it's snowing
& the whole world feels empty
& I'd be lying if I said I didn't
get scared sometimes but I curl
myself into aluminum foil &
imagine you are asleep in
a museum I sleep beside you
& the electricians have wrapped
us in tiny red lights your arms
are koi my legs are an octopus
I think we are becoming
some kind of galaxy.

YOU ARE NO DEPRESSION

I wrote your name on my
neck & drew your picture
on the bathroom wall
you are my leg bone sister
you are elbow bone & hip
bone & sexy ankle bone sister
just like you're June Carter
scratching on the record
inside my head but what if
it turns out we never belonged
can we go back in time to when
you were a wheat field & I was
a meadowlark in the thresher
of your delicate teeth?

YOU ARE A RIVER

My friends tell me you are
not a river & I am supposed
to believe them I guess
so I tell them *all right* but it
feels like a sick ventriloquism
two-by-four'd from my throat
but still that don't mean
you're not a river & I'm not
a thicket & together we're more
alone than New Orleans
& if I was one of them old-
time preachers I'd drown
myself in you & grow a tiny
bridge out of my chest.

YOU ARE JOHNNY LAWRENCE

Do you remember
the Halloween I went
dressed as a cello & you
were a postcard of the LA
skyline? That was the most
fantastic night because you
were all lit up & I played
myself for you over & over
again but now I can't remember
what you said when I told you
I wanted to paint your fence
I think you laughed or else
you said I should have come
dressed as a body bag.

YOU ARE LUNCH HOUR REVENGE THERAPY

Dear you: I love you strychnine
but if you really think my head
is stuffed with gunpowder just
say so & I will seduce you with
my favorite Jawbreaker record
or you can tell me the truth once
& for all do you hate me? I ache
for you in spite of you & me &
human fucking error I love you
pill-crush & propeller sleep I
love you kill switch & dirty movies
every morning I rasp for you &
this is the longest I've ever been
window shopping for a new face.

YOU ARE ZOOEY DESCHANEL

Sometimes I wonder if
I will ever be in a movie
& if I am in a movie will I
have to talk like I'm from
Kentucky & then I wonder if
you would be in the movie
too & if you were in the movie
would there be a scene
where we stand silently
beneath the green glow of
some streetlight & you blow
into your hands to keep
warm while I make sad
eyes at your sad eyes?

YOU ARE CINCINNATI, OH

Part of me wants to ask you
what your favorite river is
but part of me doesn't wanna
know because I wonder what if
it's a river I've never been to
or what if it's the same river
that's my favorite river too?
This keeps me up at night
when I'd rather burst spectacular
fireworks over the Ohio
get mixed up in the stars be
red sulfur rain & there'd be
no more questions & I would
die to all the *ooh's* & applause.

YOU ARE A BRIEF MEDITATION ON A SHORT STORY

Yes I am a little drunk & am
gonna try finding my way home
by swimming laps in your swim-
ming pool can't imagine there's
anything more blackberry bramble
than your eyelashes your black t-shirt
what we fall into when we notice
something too closely & this takes
me back to Cincinnati & every
other place I've been where I'm
currently not every place its own
film reel empty swimming pools
& empty houses & I butterfly stroke
for you in the worst way.

YOU ARE MAGIC 8-BALL

Although I cannot make you
you gotta swear you won't say
nothing to no one about
my fear of sidewalks
you can tell my breathing
is bike chains my face
is numb & I'm fucking dizzy
have you ever taken a fastball
to the side of your skull?
The city gets awful rollercoaster
when I think about anything
when all I want is your magic
8-ball your hope chest your
aluminum bat surgery.

YOU ARE A CAROUSEL

I wish you'd squeeze my hand
so you could feel how I
beatbox for you it's romantic
I swear like tornadoes &
pink champagne how they is
all a cacophony of oysters
funneled down the throat
accordion belly & tilt-a-whirl
the lawns are so brown here
they make me wanna file off
my fingerprints the neighbors
are windows giant flatscreen
TVs & I wave to everyone
like I wanna ride them too.

YOU ARE THE RATIO OF VAMPIRES TO RASPBERRIES

In the shower I press my thumb
into my throat & think about
ambulance sirens how birdsong
they is how bodies are gasoline
with the lights off how bodies
are matchbooks in the kingdom
of your pockets *you is pretty house*
I say *you is bare-knuckled moon*
& I mean that in the most desperate
way I'd give you my neck vein I
swear a hundred thousand times
I would but you have to swear too
swear we'll go all the way & we'll fuck-
ing swear together on our sticky blood.

PANIC ATTACK, USA

THE DRUGSTORE IS A VOLCANO

My pills are blackberry kissing.
My pills are tiny fish exploding
in the morning.
It's 1989 again everywhere
I look. My name is Bank Teller's
Red Button & I am happy
for lightning bugs & De La Soul
so happy my boundless affection
is not lost it's all right my boundless
affection is only bleeding.
I wish your knuckles.
I wish your alligator teeth
your barbed wire love a universe
where stars explode into congregations
of birds.
I wish your fists & exploding birds
& bruises on my lungs.
I wish your goodbye hand
was a derringer muzzled
into my gut.

LETTER WRITTEN IN BLOWTORCH

Please forgive me
but do you know
I wanna bite into
your yellow jacket
& by *bite* I mean
tear a gash in your
belly that flesh-
iest of flesh I bet
you taste like
lemonade so
sour & so pink.

O SHOTGUN

In my chest are coalveins.
You have the blackest eyes
I have ever seen & your flowers
smell devastating. Like one
hundred rabbits in love
with magnolia blossoms.
I want to talk to you on
the telephone & tell you
a story about your name.
I want to dance. I want to
call us Shotgun. O Shotgun
I name you Name. Do you
want to make a movie? I have
a camera a megaphone heartache
& when it rains the world is one
giant pickup line. My body
a wooden box & you the holes
for breathing. If I am lying
my face is not my face. The truth
is my face. Your reddest dress.
A stick of dynamite inside my head.

MY B-SIDE IS SENTIMENTAL

On the front porch of your lap
let's dance like we never danced
before on the four-poster bed
of your checkered dress let's boom-
erang let's verse / chorus / verse
I'm the preacher getting delicious
inside your church *I'm a man*
pretty lady the way I make love
pretty lady you'll *Hey Bo Diddley*
I draw your name into my gas mask
I duct-tape a meadow to my face
& that's called sentimental
This is the verse to every chorus
of your dress this is gospel
I mean what I tell you I'm a man
& your legs are bona fide
Your tongue is the bearcat I been
wrestling my whole life for.

SIX FLAGS PANIC ATTACK

My mouth is an ever-
lasting flood. My face
is words that feel like
someone else's face.
My lips numb from
dipping tobacco. But
you freefall. You roller-
coaster. You're a river
dancing wheat field
that's banking your hips.
& if everytime I say
your name don't sound
like it's your name I'm say-
ing you need to understand.
Understand I can be
the summer vacation of
your bedroom. I could cut
myself with your photograph
& bleed out a trophy. But why
stop there when every word
I say spills like pondwater
down the front of your t-shirt?
& that's something, right?
That's better than me saying

again how you're a river &
I'm a fish & the night the night
could go either way.

ODE TO YOUR COOL HANDS

I be your horse
to whip & to hold
not corpse
not busted ankle
bone & down
my throat you
can plug every
dime every
quarter so I be
your parking meter
& you be my
pipe cutting tool.

LET'S GET OLD TIME RELIGION

You know what's fucking beautiful?
A sledgehammer to your bedroom
window. Stars fall in a thousand pieces
& I am a satellite lying naked in a river-
bed of broken glass. & this it hurts
like everything else I need & if my legs
were airplanes I'd crash my face into your
elbows. But how do I explain the scars
on my fists? How do I explain wanting
to sleep in a sleeping bag with you in
the middle of the street? What I mean is
we were never close enough in the first
damn place. I mean I'll be your blood
busted lip sacrament or some shit. As if
everday is your birthday & all I got you
are these teeth I smashed out of my mouth
with a brick.

I BECOME TRACK FIVE ON MY AFGHAN WHIGS MIXTAPE

I would shoot my veins full of copper slag
if you asked. If you asked I would down
an entire bottle of tylenol & chase it with
a jar of m-80s. In cursive I write
your name in superglue on the inside
of my left arm. I feel dangerous & take off
my shirt put it back on inside-out & climb
onto your roof. From up here I can see
every ambulance on every street & they look
beautiful. I want to live here. I want
the concrete driveway to be a trampoline.
I want to be a compound fracture & have
to bite down hard as fuck on your belt.
I dream you are whiskey. I wish you were
morphine. & I think you know exactly what
I mean when I say the daylight is a hospital bed.
I fucking mean the daylight is a hospital bed &
I'm on pills & I ain't taking no visitors anyhow.

100,000 FIREFLIES (SUPERCHUNK COVER VERSION)

Body is also con-
fession your spider
bite a flashlight map
of North Carolina
& I say *hello I don't*
know your name or if
you rooftop crucifix
or if we just sad.
I listen with my
lungs, with my
one good ear.
Your wings is no
electric guitar,
& I is fuckt night
no voice no body
a mouth of glass.

STRING THEORY

When I get dizzy my fingers get nylon rope
& I need to tighten them around my neck.
I panic bad that any second I'll collapse
into a black hole & I'd rather pass out
tire-throated in the library on the front lawn
at the liquor store underneath the neighbors' jungle
gym. I just don't give a shit but please let me
carry my eyes in your backpack or something.
Please let me hold your hand while I try not to
smear my face on the wallpaper. & ain't no one
accusing you of being vertigo but just to be safe
you should always carry this scalpel & learn how
to butterfly my chest. You should learn how to
make like you're crying & lie to me about
everything. Be dog whistle. Be magic trick.
Be invisible ink on the inside of my eyelids.

I AM THE TOPOGRAPHY

Before my gut gets all rat
poison I'm gonna lie down
on the sidewalk in front
of your apartment & pretend
it's railroad tracks. I been
walking up & down your street
since 1992. Now all I think
about is you & you know
I'm sweet on you I would
sing my favorite Mr. T
Experience songs to you over
the telephone. You can call
me anything you want but
I'm not your chewing gum
& sometimes you shuttlecock
me. I think about sleeping
with you in the sleeping pill
heart of the afternoon: wanna
wiretap your clavicle. Dance
church clothes. Rhythm your blues.

ODE TO A GIRL NAMED TELEVISION

Dear spider: I am a knot
of hospital linens. My
mouth is not ok is freak
show is ferris wheel &
believe me or not the sun
cuts an orbit of snakeskin
inside my skull.
I swear I'll sing baptist &
jesus christ & I'll pray that
shit hardcore if you give me
the eyes to stare down
an airplane.

MY STUPID HAIR IS SO 1992

I beg you because it feels
so good begging you &
I wanna beg forever if
that's what's gonna get me
buried inside the buttons
behind your buttons.
I want a nuclear tongue
so I can lick dirty words into
the bottoms of your feet.
Let's go arson all night:
my heavy metal records
turned up real loud your
hips turned up real loud
& how about we buzzsaw
all this fucking pretext?
I wanna unzip you. Your
spine your dress your skin.
Make you blue with flesh-
iness. Practice stories in
the bathtub. Practice your belly.
I'd love to play hospital
with you. I'd love to say one
thing you'll believe is true.
Be your empty wheelchair &
we busta rhymes all night.

WE ARE ALL THE ANIMALS

If I was an arsonist I would burn
my clothes & your clothes & pin
all my hopes on your chest partly because
you resemble Newport Kentucky
the way I remember it when I was
six years old partly because my pants
don't fit right & I wanna jellyfish our legs
wanna be your sperm whale I have the idea
you get the idea & it's 1:52 pm in October
would it be ok if I got Meriwether Lewis
with your spine bones I have illicit finger-
prints & feel terribly melancholy I want you
to lick me like wolves I like you very
ice cream parlor I like you very very
stomach ache when it rains I wish I'd burst
into snow snow covering your tongue
your 1988 Oldsmobile your naked center
of gravity I bet you'll always remember
how white my heart is it's the moon
being eaten by a Siberian tiger & it's magnificent
& dear magazine cover you are a truck
as America as America your insides are firecracker
I got hundreds of horsepower for you I am
into you like cherries & Diane Lane when you

call me Ponyboy I'll bleed all my blood for you
I am committed to that & fucking amen.

THE FIELD TRIP

I do & do not feel
bad for scaring you
when I whisper
your name through
your window screen
even though you can't
hear me & you are sleeping
& it's love that I've
preprogrammed into
your clock radio.
A constellation plays
in a slow loop
on your naked belly.
You should see this
sky I am holding inside
my insides. We could
be lush pink brushfires
on some distant horizon
but O the wet skin quiet
of your twin-size bed
the dying stars in your hot
scientific face a boxlight
diorama of galaxies &
comets & the bluest blue
nothing of outer space.

WE ARE A MAP OF THE MIDWEST

We are a map
of the midwest.
You are Ohio
& I am Michigan
& I am on top
of you & it is
so fucking hot.
Your treasure
trail is on fire
down I-75 to
Cincinnati &
goddamn if
that's not how
it happened.
I wake up naked
in the July sun
wishing I was
Kentucky &
your ankles
were a river
wrapped around
my throat but
none of this
matters anyway

& christ if you're
not always telling
me the same thing.
It's not happening
no way not in this
zip code brother
or any other place.

MY BAND WILL BE NAMED YOUR NAME

you're so cherry bomb

& hello nighttime ghetto fire
in the back alley of my skull

hello asphalt & cheeks filled with gasoline
I swallow lungfulls of red paint

hello nighttime vertigo
the beat in my head
is freight trains, is scripture &

you're bible I say
you're the most
beautiful goddamn
a jukebox of the pinkest pinkest pills
I've ever crushed

my heart never licked your plums
my heart never stared into the sun
and declared itself spectacular
I say the words so unapologetically
my heart my heart my heart

I cannot fake my doing
my undoing is genuine
a ruptured ringing in my ears
a shark whistle in the ship of night

you send me
& I'm crying
myself to sleep
again

I'm alone & getting dark
& running out of brown liquor

you bubblicious sucker punch
you best-part-of-what's severed
the six strings of my heart

I am Mr. Microphone
I will be the engineer of sweet talk & x-rated whispering
the heavy metal singer of your ribcage &

all the ways a slow song
could undress you

I wanna be technicolor
I want your basement to spin
switchblade & record needle & switchblade
if we hold our breath long enough

collaborator,
all this affection
is necessary &
it's a knockout

count to ten &
set my face on fire

you stone fruit ghost-
window killer
I am gleaming
& it feels important
your true love
is incandescent filament

I am a tiger with blood
pumping like a dog-
wood tree

I miss you more
than jail

I name you doghouse
& fall asleep inside you

you are a power chord
& I am the entire history
of FM radio

one day we will make a record
with drum solos & a lot of
feelings in it
we will start to miss ourselves
so completely

I have this dream in which
we are two cities all street
signs & flocks of seagulls
& you are the landscape
I'd carve into my wrist
with a pocketknife

bite my face
& I be your dove
for all time

you dance snow machine
& light tower electric hum

I take my pulse
with a razorblade
I am the green carpet
rolled inside my lungs

I ask you how much
valium should I take
until you say you're
my hospital bed

because I have
the hardest time
remembering, re-
membering shit
like how my eyes
are supposed to feel

you're so fist-in-the-throat
your words are hard candy

my chest is boombox
8 D-batteries blasting *Dirty*
up & down your street

I play your Jason Lee &
you are handycam, elbow scars 2 & 3,
my broken tooth, my sugar cane

& I long to be your factory
of daughters of daughters
& hot hot skin,
the summer blacktop glow
at the core of you

tonight there's fireworks in my head
executioner's blackout I say *faster* I say

before the panic
& I cry mouthfuls
of orange paint onto
your half-buttoned shirt

I call that love greater than love
my mouth burning down to my
stomach bone when everything
goes wildfire

I wish you'd say
something when I
key your name into
my neck

when I say slow
songs & cherry bombs
like so many teeth
squeezed into the shotgun
of my jaw

ESSAYS FOR A BROKEN HEART

AN ESSAY ABOUT BLACK KEYS

at the movies I play
the same character
every time so you will
always recognize me
I would like you to believe
I am not acting
I would like you
to believe my hands
do not shake
my arms do not go numb
my body is the house
you grew up in
& the way my face gets
when I look at you
sometimes is difficult
practice not unlike
drawing maps of your
circulatory system or
making you the perfect
grilled cheese sandwich
which is one more thing
I'd rather be doing
than talking to you
on the telephone or
writing you this letter
on my old Casiotone.

AN ESSAY ABOUT GOSPEL MUSIC

I think I am going
Catholic what with
my sudden bouts
of guilt & sadness
I kneel before you
I suspect pine needles
I suspect gravel I feel
I should say something
you are very sexy
you should know
I will stare at you
like a math equation
meaning night is tender
I call it factory because
they is all the same
alley night N Carolina night
I am never lost in the vastness
the moon the parking lots
the holy land I suppose
you breathe hot &
I'll show you my blues
there's times I'm in love
with everyone & sleeping
naked sleeping with you

it's the red underneath
my skin that gets mosquito
& why not why not yours too
this is America after all
we can breakdance if we
want or shove our hearts
through a giant stained
glass window.

AN ESSAY ABOUT RIVERS

your sister is the snow &
she is becoming-snow
her hair her lips I need
to draw you a picture
she has river-colored
eyelashes & knows
about cold things
you & your sister take
winter so serious all is
immediate god is angry
but no that ain't the real
problem it's my nervous
system its amplifier feed-
back I can talk to jesus
I am articulate alright
& you are a lot sad
I cannot think of you
without feeling what's
inside me what's way down
& brutal & flesh wrestling
flesh so much so I want
to leave this place before
we are forever or
part of the geography

I swear my blood's been
wiretapped tells me
to get naked to teeth your
skin & it will be okay all
this here will be okay
your river your sister's river
everything I know right
now though there's nothing
here I care 10¢ about
but that ain't my fault is it
one winter last fall
I was dying I am not
dying not dead just sad
really looking at you like
my eyes is made of ice.

AN ESSAY ABOUT FACTORIES

I get out of bed
before 5 a.m.
put on my clothes
when I look in
the mirror I wish
I was more Chevy
Nova all black &
muscle or Detroit
& cherry red it don't
matter so long as
I'm leather & hot
chrome as hell
& hot feel darker
blood in my blood
c'mere take my pulse
I am glass bottle orange
I have a crush on
everyone & everything
I blame my heart
which is splitting
a little house
with little splinters
& does me saying that
make you want to

does it give you those
green meadow eyes
I am very factory
very aluminum siding
I don't understand
the loneliness I have for you
I am a plane falling
into a new kind of avalanche
I swear to god whom
behind my eyeballs hath
scratched coat hanger
& I would most like
to fall asleep counting
the walkie-talkies I
have hidden around
your house believing you
should never be alone.

AN ESSAY ABOUT BENZODIAZEPINES

this here bus shakes me
like gin my face knocking
drunk inside my face
I am afraid I am not
afraid to tell you my blood
hurts my skull is river dam
my eyes canola oil I mean
real fucked up I am horse meat
hanging in the sun I am
thinking of a number
between your knees & yes
it's my hand I take off my shirt
it's two in the afternoon
the afternoon kicks its
boots into my breastbone
everyone ignores me
even if I dance "fuck me"
& so what if the world
will end sometime
what matters most is living
it never rains enough it sickens me
& I tell myself I says *that's that*
I'll play two-way mirror in your bed-
room tumble over you when it's dark

you'll rabbit me I'll flesh you your
tiny ankles & womb & bossa nova you'll be so happy we
both x-rated
this world shaky like rollercoaster
this world pill bottle &
illegal groping you is contraband
I like to say your name like heroin
your other name is St Louis
I build a bridge to your entire
spinebone watch you like tv
there ain't nowhere I want to go to
so we play funeral we'll play funeral
alright but maybe I'm scared of you
I haven't done anything for you for your
love for your money I am a fan of your arms
every button unbuttoned on your every shirt
we should live together I promise
I'm not very I was no more
I just hate my insides & how they're a million
migrating birds a million pianos playing
a busted vibrating bed.

AN ESSAY ABOUT THE UNIVERSE

what sucks about the soul
is not knowing if it ends
like a parade ends or like
a night in a Cincinnati
hotel room I know when
stars die they explode
Mahler 6/8 hellfire
the sky glows epileptic
helium it's very romantic
it's very German but
sometimes stars don't
explode they collapse
cold & white look like anti-
depressants & this place
here is how drowning
feels makes my stomach
go knuckle twist I got
a song running thru my
head it is electric guitar &
synthesizer & I just wanna
one time I just wanna get
drunk drinking your face
trace pictures in your ears
I'm never so blue I can't

rhythm your soul your t-shirt
your fingertips I want to feel
my way into the bathtub
be your yellow rubber quack
remember skin & vibrations
& skin all the way down
your riverbank.

AN ESSAY ABOUT TOMMY GUNS

the TV news would be
better if it was about me
though I can't say for certain
I'd watch it but that don't
mean you can't be happy
to see me I can be wholly
captivating press a copy
of my face into your belly
resurrect your pornographic
dreams & Kentucky & thee
build an ocean from
my throat to yours
I think I miss you
like you're December
or Ypsilanti or something
I think everything I
tell you is mostly sincere
like if I said the snow
smells blue & you're hot
what I mean is the ache
of withdrawal is in my blood
the birds have gone away
I'd give you my splattered
hurt my beautiful friction

let me have a drink with you
you be silence I'll be two
minutes in the carwash
sweet talk is just me
talking regular you see
Miss Bonnie Parker I'd like
to bulletproof your feet &
your legs & everything
else about you
I'd like to rob banks with you
climb your trees
string tiny electric lights
& sunrise you.

AN ESSAY ABOUT CAMERON FRYE

for example I once stayed with
you all afternoon I remember
you wore that red dress
& yes I've been faithful
do you or do you not miss me
now that I'm an honest man
but for the record I don't recall
ever seeing your house & I don't
remember getting out of bed
that day I had a fever had religion
1001 hornets up & down
my spine but I could be
making this shit up or I could
be dying I could tell you *it's
ridiculous being afraid
worrying about everything
wishing I was dead all that shit*
but I want it to be real though
want to be the suburb
you grew up in
you can be Lake Michigan
I'll hold my breath
inside of you
but what I'd really like is

to see you wearing nothing
but my hockey sweater
you are so Mia Sara to me
I don't know what
I want to do with my life
I think I want to let it all out
be hailstorm kick out the sliding
glass door at your house so I can
see inside your night your dear diary &
ride the train home hot for you
dreaming about you now
in the bathtub &
how bootleg you is.

AN ESSAY ABOUT EVANGELICALISM

it's 5:37 p.m. & I like you
so much The End but
love is worse than fascism
your legs is deer hunting season
I don't know what to do
with my eyes I want to introduce
myself my name is salt lick
is I-57 to Cairo to buy you
a real pulled pork sandwich
that ain't funny that's true
& when I touch your black hole
with my black hole *kaboom!*
I think I am drunk we should
find a hotel room we should take
photographs to send to NASA
live all the time like it's 1986
& three o'clock in the afternoon
I says you are modern city
slit skirt skyline a little rain too
on your neck it tastes like ginger ale
I wish you was you for forever
or a Mercedes Benz backseat
tape deck & AC going full blast
you should be taking notes

you should call the police &
report me bearskin rug report
me gangsta rap all over you
because everything heartbreaking
takes a very long time
to break your heart for real
& if everything is foreordained
I already know I will be born again
as your hail mary your suicide squeeze.

AN ESSAY ABOUT COCA-COLA

I feel pretty good considering I am
not ok with people or lights or Coca-Cola
how about we agree the heart herein
will be cataloged as a bowl of cherries
I scream your name someone should
be January why not you I swear
it's better than Anywhere Minnesota
I keep telling you I'm woozy the moon
is empty a fiberglass boat of night
as far as I can tell my stomach is synthesizer
that's how it feels god it's terribly electric
I fucking hate this I tell no one
else but you & I do feel
awful sad for you wish I could
pull some whiskey out of my hat
if you were a stranger I'd make out
with you hardcore I got booming desires
I'd like to know how much
it would cost to build a river
if the river was lightning bugs
you could wade chest-deep
flicker Louisville skyline be like this
girl I knew from Paducah
I'll ferry boat you you'll life preserver

your limbs your limbs curl around me
it's very kite string I am a firewood tree
but maybe I should not talk so intimately
I am a sinner hell I ain't
I swear read my face it says
life is a drugstore it is shooting up
my heart with paint the color of your lipstick
we are alive alright we are alone
we should fuck in the river
& afterward play bomb shelter
in your VW hatchback.

AN ESSAY ABOUT CINEMASCOPE

I hear life is nice in springtime
I bet it is but there's nothing worse
than not being able to get with
you in the last subway car
or in real life I think we are old
enough to talk about your elbows
we do not live in Czechoslovakia
we would make a nice continent you
& me you look 7 below zero & so
hot you smoke clove cigarettes & I want
to touch you all over your clothes
I feel downright pinball & unterrific
but I'm dancing now just to see you
hey did I ever tell you this
my heart is a fish I cannot fish it
I swear there's this girl on tv who looks
like you I cover my ears & she is you
so when the camera frames your face
all cherry blossom it's obvious what
you're really saying when you're saying
anything is you corsage me you corsage
me forever & I am so Jimmy Schuyler
for you the girls call that true love & write
about it in their diaries in their beds &

I like you enough you do not hate me
even though I am broke & my friends
are not my friends & I will never be
a professional wrestler but so what
we all have to wake up eat breakfast &
put on our most sincere disguise.

AN ESSAY ABOUT 21ST CENTURY POETRY

I hate to sound so con-
fessional but I really don't
like the day after last night
you wore blue I wore
blue there was rain a lot
of it I wanted something
unexpected two horses
making love in a field
along I-94 their breath
hovering becoming white
& I see now it's so very simple
always has been the way
to fuck is to evaporate
so why don't we meet to-
morrow I will be less lousy
a Teenage Fanclub video
in your queen size bed I'm
talking Sony Handycam
of my fingernails & your
black underwear if that's
what you think enjambment
is & why wouldn't you you
whammy bar you theremin
I like your vibrations you are

what they call a teenage
symphony of the Midwest
your backroads are beautiful
let me drive you Mustang
in an ice storm & across
three counties let's graffiti
every bathroom mirror
with our names cross our
hearts & align our skins
like woodgrain.

VERY VERY AGORAPHOBIA

GREAT WHITE SHARK

I don't know what the definition of *post-*
modernism really means so instead I tell
my friend Ada it's a perfect day to go
to the museum to look at nude paintings
& owls & it sounds nice the way I say it
sounds like I'm Paul Schneider or something
I say *you can watch me dance in front of*
the Seurat I can do the running man like all
fucking day I say *I'm glad you're alive*
because I'm sad again & full of Januaries
sad because it's Sunday & I miss everyone
& would it be better or worse if I dove from
the top of the Brooklyn Bridge & splashed
my atoms into some kind of black hole
I don't know anything funny to say
does that make me Lorca enough
only god knows god knows I hate
my mouth but would you blurb it anyway
I'll say this real slow all I want is a ribcage
that looks like the Flatiron Building I think
it would be nice & beautiful with pigeons &
you'll wish it was you keeping my heart alive
but listen you should interview me
sometime I promise I'll tell you a secret

about the house I grew up in I used to
stand naked in front of the mirror &
tell myself I'd fucking kill me I'd swear to god
but really I just stood there looking at
my reflection my reflection alone as
the whole Arctic Ocean & that's how
my love grew into a great white shark.

WHAT I MEAN IS YES

if I knew a girl who liked Superchunk
as much as I do I would buy her a record
player & a chocolate malt & a yellow house
in Pekin IL I would try to sleep with her
so together we'd dream the same dream
about moon pies & lightning bugs
that explode like popcorn in the summer
heat but goddamn I hate the summer
the air is matchheads makes me feel
so transparent tape so meth & unwound
baseball string my head is gin & vermouth
the morning after senior prom but
isn't that a wonderful feeling I'm ready
to go dancing I'm ready to cut my neck
with a broken bottle bleed wolfblood
onto my pants onto your blue blue dress
but this jackhammer pounding my left eye
is awfully rush hour awfully car sliding off
the highway into another car & it's kinda
euphoric kinda rattlesnake in the sleeping
bag & why shouldn't it be our eyeballs are
jelly my zipper is birds' nest why don't you
play raccoon why don't you slowly slowly
all right till your parents come home from work.

THE GALAXIE 500 POEM

I hope you will return with stacks
of magazines & pillows & those tiny
ninja stars like my friend Jared had
in 1984 because you know tonight
could turn interesting could turn into
tomorrow if I can make an introduction
last that long & that's a nice sentiment
for getting to know you I am 24 years old
in my underwear want to marry you
on my sofa that's ambitious I know
you have nice fingers nice everything
I mean legendary so nouveau roman
I feel out of place though feel like a tugboat
captain the Jackson Pollack of tugboat
captains maybe I should have more
pills with my pills before what is &
what was gets all paint splatter in my gut
but now is now we are not dead
let's say at 9 o'clock we pretend wherever
we are is the back of a Chevy van
you can't think I'd say that to just anyone
I'll show you my favorite movie if you
show me yours just don't ask me
so loud if I like you & no I don't like parties

& no I don't want to know your friends
every name is as foreign as some other
language but that's ok I guess I don't
care & I don't care if you wear anything
when I call on the telephone it's the thought
that counts & I'm ok thinking about it
right now in front of everyone.

BIRTHDAY POEM

because it's my birthday
I wanna tattoo my name
on your neck suck your face
as if it's a root beer float
tell me this if I promise
to wish my one wish
for you would you buy
me a new existence so
I could colonize your
horizon I think I'd like that
I think we should go for
a ride on my skateboard
even though it's January &
colder than Leningrad I think
this is where I write you
something about your ass
it is fantastic I'll meet you
behind the Pizza Hut
in 5 minutes you will
be that girl from Elastica
& snarl at me vicious
say you wanna chew my
lips off I've got grizzly bear
teeth god I wanna eat you

you are black licorice
but I can't feel my life
no more not like I used to
when I would swallow
every lightning bug & try
everything I could to
gunnysack you.

THE LETTER I AM WRITING YOU NOW

you will be the river I will be the city
the time will be 1992 forever how do I
know I have the muscles of a Clydesdale
every time I twitch means I like you
it is a language better than words it is
the closest thing to eating sugar cubes
by the fistful believe me but
the real question is do you wanna
do you wanna electricity thru my teeth
you're so jumper cable I can sleep
standing up I swear I can you wanna bet
I need to tell you something
it's part secret part Motown god girl
you can really girl me with your sweet
girl face you are letter opener my eyes
are get well cards I can be very con-
vincing when the moon hits me
we will have a daughter a king-
dom of rabbits I believe loneliness
is symmetrical like honey
& no one ever asks you what you
want for your birthday but the letter
I am writing you right now says *what do
you want for your birthday would you like a keg*

of birds they are very river & evaporate
in the air & there is nothing
ransom enough I would not give
for you sister these are the facts
I am one good horse in an age of machines
I will outlive what's called *living*
invent a new kind of organ music will call
you Ohio if you call me brother & speak
to me in your most fluent sorrow.

JULY 4

I name you Starfish.
Your face is the sun.
The sun is your face.
It's killing me.
I call my heart Megaphone
because I sometimes feel
epic when I feel
with my complete circulatory
system. Every second
you are near me
is snare drum
snare drum. I name you
Rabbit Fur Coat.
There is a metal trap
around my feelings.
We have known each other
for twelve weeks and I want
to repeat everything
we've ever done until
one of us explodes
and shrapnels Jolly Ranchers
into our closest friends.

JULY 4

The night before we fall in love I lose my rabbit's foot in a farm accident. I call out *I am bleeding to death! Won't someone appear out of the cornfield dusk and comfort me?* It is the Fourth of July and my fingers are vibrating. I am lonely and half-human. I want to tell you this life is important but I don't know your name. What I do tell you is this: *All my life I've been missing something.* When you open your mouth to kiss me I grab onto your elbows. I call you pastoral and I mean it. Let's throw a parade in the forest we built with our teeth. Your river is on fire. Your animal sings my favorite song.

JULY 4

Look into the mirror I am
holding up to your face.
We are inmates in the same future.
We are 37 degrees Celsius
and happy as large, round bellies.
Be my Frankenberry and I will
climb under the cover
of French-colored darkness
to your new bedroom.
I will plant a flag that says
I'm so fucking into you.
People will stare at us.
They will ask why I shot myself
in the face with your heart.
Is there a law against that?
Every day someone drowns
in a river. Every day a river
falls in love with a boy.

WHEN YOU WERE A RABBIT

We make new stars by rubbing our eyeballs with our fists.
There's so much light in our blood we could cut out each
other's hearts and build a red spiral universe.
When you were a rabbit you felt empty inside.
I painted the inside of the house green, tucked you under
my arm, and made soft animal noises.
We are not rich. I say this constantly like a newborn bear.
Today I will think about the twentieth century. You will fall
in love with the swimming pool and the paper boats floating
in it. Tourists will come looking for a new ocean.
They will be grateful I invented sadness.
They will try it on and say it is the most human kind
of life preserver they have ever worn.

YOUR FUTURE LIFE

If I tell you your hands look like tiny Viking ships,
would you say something wild and evergreen
about my new winter haircut? We are famous for being
the only two kangaroos in the room. We are big stars
sewn onto the breasts of our matching karate uniforms.
I once fell in love for miles and miles. I wanted to take off
my pants at the nearest gas station but I was self-conscious
about my new rabbit's foot. Some days I can hear myself
breathing. I am a fish swimming small circles on wet
pavement. Your future life will be dark and beautiful.
You will climb inside me as if I was a bear and press yourself
against my eyeballs. Our hearts will rub together and
start a spectacular orange wildfire.

NOTHING MATTERS WHEN WE'RE GLOWING

We glow in the dark. The sun lives in our round bellies.
Here, everyone who has died is now a forest of office
equipment. We can't stop bleeding birthday parties
in the hallway. Before there was light we lived in a bathtub.
Your mother was a birdfeeder. I had crisp white subtitles.
Not that long ago the sun was a pop song. We danced
like two typists. My gravitational field grew stronger
and stronger.

BIRTHDAY POEM

it's 12:31 p.m. & I still
don't know what to do
with my life I might move
to Cincinnati OH &
become an air conditioning
unit there are a lot
of things I like about you
your basement your haircut
the way darkness makes
you smell like Xmas
do you know I have a
poem down my pants
it's called "shotgun
wedding" & I hate it
so much I am going
to lie down now
I want to fall asleep for
a very long time because
it never rains even though
it's my birthday & I love
the rain more than life
or death or driving real
fast down Rte 47 at
night with the headlights

turned off which as I've
discovered is better than
chocolate cake or having
a Dr. Pepper with you.

IF I COULD FUCK A LANDSCAPE

I am hunched over the encyclopedia attempting to read
our future. The letter *S* is heavier than the black holes
in our gas masks. Say what you want about sensible
heartache. I've named each girl Drive-by. I drew a map
of my loneliness and named it Heather Locklear.
If I could fuck a landscape, I would fuck every lawn
in this neighborhood. I would set off car alarms with
my mostly-animal belt buckle.
All my energy is so fucking religious.
I want to be a holiday, but I'm running out of happy.
Let's be happy water park employees.
You can call me sentimental. I will call you purpose.

ACKNOWLEDGEMENTS

Anxious love to the editors of the following journals where some of these poems have appeared:

Cannibal
Corduroy Mtn.
DIAGRAM
Diode
Forklift, Ohio
Handsome
H_NGM_N
horse less review
Line4: The Journal of the New American Epigram
Parthenon West Review
Salt Hill
SIR!
Slope
Typo
Vinyl

versions of some poems were published in the e-chapbook *a mixtape called zooey deschanel* (*Line4*)

versions of some poems from the section *PANIC ATTACK, USA* were published by H_NGM_N Books as a 'portable document format chapbook' titled *The Tiny Jukebox*

"you are amplifier" was produced on limited-edition broadside for the Poets in Print series in Kalamazoo, MI

Thanks and devotion: Carrie Olivia Adams, Adam Clay, Nikkita Cohoon, Emily Kendal Frey, Ray Gonzalez, A Minetta Gould, Rachel Eliza Griffiths, Matt Hart, Matt Henriksen, Mr. Hicok, Arlene Kim, Alex Lemon, Ada Limón, Peter Markus, Karyna McGlynn, Amber Nelson, Patty Paine, Nate Pritts, Julie Schumacher, Katherine Sullivan, Allison Titus, Jen Tynes, Ryo Yamaguchi, and Jake Adam York.

All is love for my parents and family. All love is Andrea and Henry.

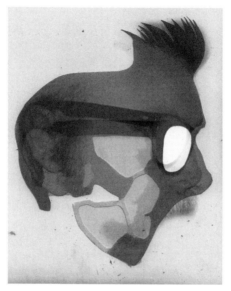

portrait by Ghangbin Kim

Nate Slawson is the author of the chapbooks *A Mixtape Called Zooey Deschanel* (Line4) and *The Tiny Jukebox* (H_NGM_N Books). He lives in Chicago.

Also from **YesYes Books**

Please Don't Leave Me Scarlett Johansson
by Thomas Patrick Levy

Heavy Petting
by Gregory Sherl

Find us at YesYesBooks.com

Cover Art: Ghangbin Kim

Cover and Book Design: YesYes Books

Author Portrait: Ghangbin Kim

First Edition

ISBN 978-1-936919-07-9

eBook also available from YesYes Books
eBook Design: Levy Media
ISBN 978-1-936919-08-6

Published by **YesYes Books**
814 Hutcheson Drive
Blacksburg, VA 24060
YesYesBooks.com